# Ladypreneur®
# Code

## Rules of Engagement for Women in Business

Juanika Dildy

Ladypreneur Academy, LLC.
Richmond, VA 23228
www.theladypreneur.com

ISBN: 978-0-9992468-0-1

# Introduction

*"To all the ladies in the place with style and grace…"*

This is my favorite quote from the late Notorious B.I.G. Why? It addresses a certain type of female. The one with style and grace. The one with poise and excellence. The one with positive intent and ambition. The one with character and confidence. The one with goals and strategy. The Ladypreneur.

Ladypreneur® (lédi-prənə́r): the ultimate female entrepreneur.

I could bore you with a list of degrees, credentials, and experience as qualifiers for writing this book, but that's not what I want you to remember. No matter your level in business, I've likely been where you are. Successes and failures, wins and losses, joy and pain, faith and sometimes fear make up the story of my life. But it's important to note that God is not a waster, and all things eventually worked out for my good! There is work to be done, lives to be changed, atmospheres to be shifted, treasure to be gained, and

I'm on a mission to equip the women of the world to make it happen. God made us "helpers" because he knew we could get the job done.

As for the golden rule, Thou Shalt Make Her Own Money!

I encourage you to use what's in your hand. What talent or skill have you been blessed with to make a difference in your own way? I challenge you to work it. That idea, that book, that blog, that artwork, that recipe, that design, those clothes. Whatever it may be, make it a hustle and monetize your passion!

Join me, as together we unlock *The Ladypreneur®* *Code, Rules of Engagement for Women in Business.*

# Table of Contents

# 1

# First Things First

Ok ladies (and gentlemen), how many of you have the desire to be successful in business but have no idea where to start? I remember being in your exact shoes, just a size 7.5. I'd spent many years in corporate America, not realizing that every experience in life conditions you with a certain mindset that forms your expectations. What do I mean by this? Well, I'd never been an entrepreneur, so I didn't know how to walk, talk, think, or behave like one.

If I can take it all the way back, as I child, I grew up with parents that taught me the value of things with the unintentional effect of making some of it mentally out of reach. Many of you that grew up in households similar to mine can easily finish the phrases, "money doesn't grow on…trees," or "money is the root of all…evil."

Now I'm not knocking this philosophy because no one wants a spoiled child, but I can guarantee that none of us, even me in my adulthood, realized the mental impact we have on impressionable minds when we tell them what they can't or shouldn't do, especially when it comes to finances.

Needless to say, this was one of the first things that I'd have to unlearn. Little did I know, the impact of constantly hearing how money is limited and that a camel could fit through the eye of a needle before a rich man could get into heaven made me question just how much success I wanted. I never doubted my potential, but a fear of flying can keep you pretty low to the ground.

Now, speaking of conditioning, it didn't stop at home. For the bulk of my life, I was conditioned to time. I had to wake up at a certain time to be at school at a certain time. We ate lunch at a certain time and switched classes at a certain time every single day. Even when school ended, the conditioning continued.

I still had to be at work by a certain time, took breaks at a certain time, and ate lunch at a certain time. I was so used to being told what to do and when to do it, I struggled with entrepreneurship. As a business owner, I'd be responsible for setting and sticking to my schedule. But, there were no detention days or write ups if I fell short, the consequences were all my own.

Similarly, as an entrepreneur, I'd no longer be handed objectives, curricula, or told what to do. I'd be responsible for determining what work was needed and how to implement it. There was also nothing to hold me accountable for what I did or didn't get done. Again, the consequences and motivation all fell on me.

This can be tough for someone that's been conditioned as the worker bee and not the queen. No matter how you may see yourself, if you've experienced this conditioning, there are certain behaviors that you'll need to unlearn before you can achieve, but more importantly, maintain success. You see ladies; wealth is a mindset. We've all seen people hit the lottery or become an overnight success, and before you know it, they're broke again! Don't let this be you. Take the time to invest in your most profitable asset, your mindset. Trust me; it's going to take a different thought pattern to keep going when no one is pushing you. It'll take a different mindset to rebuild what you've lost. It takes a certain skill to see what others can't see and do what others won't do.

So, let's get started. First things first:

Figure out why you're taking this journey in the first place. I'd like to think of WHY as an acronym for What Has You. What has you up early in the morning or up late at night? What's the one thing you can't shake if you tried? Is it a passion for an idea that can change the world? Is it the desire to give back? Is it retiring a spouse or sending a child to college, debt free? Is it the ability to travel and live the lifestyle you've always wanted? Is it the satisfaction of success and accomplishing that which has been tugging on your heart? Why do you want to be an entrepreneur?

Whatever the answer, please make sure that it's larger than money. Why? Because money that we've never had isn't enough to keep us on a path of discomfort. Hear me clearly; ENTREPRENEUR-SHIP IS UNCOMFORTABLE! It can be scary, risky, difficult, and stretching. Therefore, your desired outcome has to mean enough to you to keep you in the game, even when it hurts, when you feel you've failed, or when it costs you money!

Now that we've covered some of the basics, let's cover the rules of engagement for women in business.

Juanika Dildy

# Thoughts

# 2

# Authentically
# YOUnique

There's a common misconception in the business world that to be successful, you must "become." Don't get me wrong, growth is necessary for anything to survive, but not at the expense of sacrificing its authenticity. So many business owners spend so much time and energy trying to become something, they lose sight of what they are already. You attract who you are, and to maintain that attraction, in the long run, it must be consistent. Here's the catch, fake always becomes faulty, and it's impossible to remain consistent where you're constantly forced to recreate.

Case in point, I'm a Beyoncé fan; a REAL fan. I have every album and I know every song. This alone qualifies me as an expert for this theory. Over the past 20 years, we've seen change occur in Beyoncé's career. Her sound changed, her moves changed, and her lyrics changed. However, in the midst of this evolution, we only witnessed a consistent enhancement of Beyoncé's brand, not a continuous recreation. What do I mean? There's always a consistent "it girl" theme to every phase of her life that was represented in her music. We saw her start off with her friends, communicating "it girl" confidence and independence. We then saw her break out as the leader of those friends, establishing herself as the "it girl" image with the "it girl" work ethic. Later, we experienced "it girl" independence in the introduction of her solo career. That later turned into the "it girl" wife and the "it girl" mom.

Get my point? Things will always change, but the underlying theme must remain consistently authentic. I challenge you today to determine an underlying theme that is unique to you and your business. This underlying theme will ultimately become your BRAND, so take time to think about it. Ask yourself the following questions:

- What am I known for?
- What do I do best?
- What best represents me?
- How would I describe my business?
- What need am I filling?

The answers to these questions will help you to determine a brand that will grow with you as you evolve as a business owner. Take the time to write down your answers and layout a brand plan that encompasses both your current realm of business and your goals. When you've completed the exercise, let's focus on Rule #2: Be Specific.

# Thoughts

# 3

# **Be Specific**

W e've all heard the phrase, "a confused mind does nothing." This is true in all aspects. A confused brand won't sell. A confused company won't produce. A confused customer certainly won't buy. In other words, confusion will always kill productivity.

My first area of business was in network marketing. I'm well aware of how many people knock the industry, but it's the safest place to learn entrepreneurship with minimal risk. Here, I was responsible for leading a team to recruit both customers and business partners. After years of success peaks and valleys, I noticed that every single time confusion increased, productivity decreased. It's no different in traditional business, so take the time to provide clarity.

The first thing that requires clarity is your purpose. You need to know what you're doing and why you're doing it. If you're just getting started in business, here's the easiest way to determine it. Write down the answer to the following question: **what is the need and how do I plan to meet it?**

The reason why most businesses fail is that they're unable to express its product or service in terms of meeting a need, rather than a simple offer. Please understand that a sale isn't salesy if the person is already searching for it. Have you ever seen a Facebook commercial or been contacted by an Instagram sales rep to sign up? No, why? Facebook, for example, met a unique need for social interaction, and people bought into it without much effort from the company. This is how you want to position yourself uniquely.

Next, be specific about who you're targeting. It's no secret that I'm all about the cultivation of women in business. Males are always welcome, but it's not my target. I'm certain that no man will open a book titled, Ladypreneur® Code, and be surprised that the first sentence begins with "Ok ladies." Ask yourself who you are targeting and if you'd feel any confusion if you were the buyer and not the seller.

Now, here's what's most important. Be specific on what you want to accomplish. Write this down, if you fail to plan, you can plan to fail gracefully. If you don't know where the finish line is, how will you know when you've crossed it? Do yourself a favor and plan specifically. Write down your sales goals, your reach, and financial goals, and measure yourself against them monthly.

At the beginning of each month, create a spreadsheet that lists:

- How many product sales or service hours am I targeting?
- How many people do I want to reach, or make aware of my offering?
- How many of those reached will convert to customers?
- How much money do I want to make by the end of the month?

At the end of the month, list what you've accomplished and use this to determine what should be dialed up or down. Will you need more advertising? Do you need more people entering into your sales funnel? Are you over or underpriced? Knowing how to rank against the specific monthly goals you set will help you answer each of these questions and scale your business accordingly.

Now, let's discuss the next rule of engagement: intentionality.

# Thoughts

_____

_____

_____

_____

_____

_____

_____

_____

_____

_____

_____

_____

_____

_____

_____

_____

_____

_____

_____

_____

_____

_____

Juanika Dildy

# 4

# **Be Intentional**

C ast your nets wide. I had heard it over and over during my business career and it never really sat well. It seemed like the most annoying concept, but I trusted the people that were mentoring me, so I listened.

For years I used both time and monetary resources to supply the ammunition that I'd spray at people like a machine gun. My rule was that anyone with an active pulse within a three-foot proximity would hear about what I could offer them in business. Here's the catch, the bulk of them didn't care. I was wasting bullets on people wearing protective vests, and in some cases, the responses I received felt like they were returning fire.

Then I realized, I needed a target. I had no way to measure a successful shot because I wasn't aiming at anything. Many of you have had the same experience. You've been throwing your business at "Lottie, Dottie, and everybody." It's tiring, discouraging, and wasteful. But, there's good news. The only way to achieve consistent success with a customer base is to identify a target market.

To do this effectively, you must start with you. Ask yourself the following questions:

- What do I have to offer?
- What value do I provide?
- Where have I been effective?

Now that the hard part is over, the rest should come easily to you. It may not seem difficult on paper, but the process of narrowing your intentions for clarity can be daunting. You have so many ideas, and you want to accomplish a lot. Take the time to figure out which of the cards you've been dealt can win the game, and play those. You'll see faster, more consistent results.

Now, let's focus on your target:

- Who wants what I have to offer?
- Who could benefit from what I provide?
- With whom have I experienced consistent success?

Find that lane and stay there. You'll discover that your target audience will simplify your marketing process because they only require your presence, not necessarily your promotion. You'll never have to promote what people seek, only make it available to them.

Don't forget your brand in the process. Consistency is key, and everything you do should intentionally acknowledge the underlying tone of your target audience. When you speak their language, they'll begin to listen for your voice. In other words, you won't have to chase your target. Your consistent intentionality will attract them.

Additionally, be mindful of your target's behavior patterns as you make decisions for your business. Before you place your product, think about where your target spends the most amount of time. Before you create an ad, think about what your target likes to see. Before you release information, think about when and where your target would likely receive it. Be intentional with everything in your business, and you'll no longer have to find customers because your target will search for you.

# Thoughts

_____

_____

_____

_____

_____

_____

_____

_____

_____

_____

_____

_____

_____

_____

_____

_____

_____

_____

_____

_____

_____

_____

_____

Juanika Dildy

# 5

# Act Like A Lady, Think Like A Boss

The best part about being a ladypreneur® is the simple fact that you get to be a lady in the process. Ladypreneur® defines the modern day professional woman, so be sure to balance both in your business career.

Step one, always be classy. If I could borrow a quote from a famous ladypreneur®, it would be that of Coco Chanel. Her words are music to my ears; "a woman should be two things, classy and fabulous." You see, Coco came along during a time that women weren't succeeding in free enterprise, they were only successful in self-employment. During those days, women were chefs, gardeners, seamstresses, cleaners, etc., but mostly within their own home. If they did provide work outside of their homes, goods were mainly traded and sold within their immediate community. Coco, however, had a different plan. She had an idea that would change the game for garments in her era. This breakthrough idea to make clothing out of jersey material rather than cotton was too big to keep to herself. This model gave her a seat at tables that women weren't usually welcomed, at least not as the primary guest rather than the "plus one."

The circumstances she faced didn't stop her from standing her ground. She faced businessmen and women alike with a load of confidence, but she always remained level headed and poised. Her highs were never too high, and her lows were never too low to change her stance. Class was her theme, and she practiced it well. We can all learn a lesson from Coco Chanel as we face the ups and downs of business ownership. In all things, remain classy, professional and always respond with intellect rather than emotion.

This will rid us of regret, and help to build a reputation that will sustain the life of our businesses.

Step two, dress how you'd like to be addressed. I love fashion. I believe it's a personal expression of style and personality. However, in the world of business, what you wear should complement your business and not cause a distraction. As a woman, it's important to recognize the attention that you're attracting, and what is acceptable for your business.

As a general rule, I believe that more is more. The more mindful you are of your appearance before you get dressed, the more likely you are to make an effective decision. Please don't miss my point. I'm not saying that you have to dress like a nun or a librarian. I am, however, asking that you be intentional with your impact. Every woman in the country takes a look in the mirror, does a slight dance to affirm how cute she is, and whispers the response she expects to herself before exiting. Just make sure that the response of "oh girl," "you're killing it," or "you did that" reflects the perception you'd want for yourself in the business world.

Step three, language is a locator. Let me be frank, the response you get from others is usually a reflection of your posture; and your posture is a direct reflection of your language. Years ago, I attended a women's conference where a few of my mentors were speaking. Although one mentor, in particular, was very successful, she didn't have the track record to match one of the other speakers. However, I took mental notes during the lunch panel meeting as I watched my mentor demand respect through her language. It was so sneaky but effective! The guest speaker was the last to speak before lunch, and my mentor stood up, captured everyone's attention and made the following public announcement:

> *I am so proud of how you just empowered many of the women in the room, and I must commend you for your drive and accomplishments. Most women your age want to be reality stars or video girls, but you've shown a level of professionalism that excites me, and I want everyone in the room to know how proud I am of you!*

Everyone clapped in agreement, while I chuckled inside. Did my mentor edify the guest speaker? Absolutely! But, she did it in a way that positioned her as the reigning expert. She subliminally carried the posture of a proud Auntie that had just watched her niece perform the dance moves she taught her, and it was ingenious! In other words, she "son'd" the guest speaker by giving her compliments, took back her platform, and no one noticed!

You may not always have a floor to speak, but you have the ability to use your language to boost your posture. What are some respectful pet names that you can use with people to dictate their response to you? For example, a friendly smile and a respectful name such as "sugar" or "ladybug" makes people sublimi-nally response with an attitude of "yes ma'am." For men, anything ending with "champ" makes them re-spond with an attitude of "okay coach."

I encourage you to try it. Remember to always be respectful and stay away from words that are usually used with children, like boy, girl, sweetie, or baby. These are perceived as derogatory and will likely invoke the opposite response. The key is to use your language to position yourself as the expert, but prac-tice makes perfect.

Step four, actions speak louder than words. This includes both behavior and body language. The most unfair descriptor that women are tagged with in business is "emotion." For whatever reason, our behavior and our body language say that we're emotional. Well, if you can't beat them, join them. What do I mean by this? Learn to play the game that earns you respect. Be firm in your tone, but still let your personality shine. Make it a point to remain in control of your temperament at all times. Keep a level head, and don't show your emotional side.

The best way to accomplish this is to identify your outlets up front. Find both people and activities that will allow you to blow off steam outside of the places where you'll need to demand respect. Find a friend in your workplace that you can trust enough to vent honestly. Find someone outside of your place of business that will listen with a judge-free ear, for the sake of supporting you rather than only seeking solutions. Find an activity that will free your mind momentarily. For some, it's a good workout. For others, it's a shopping spree. Whatever it is for you, make time for it to help balance your emotions.

# Thoughts

Juanika Dildy

# 6

# Use What You've Learned

One of the most detrimental mistakes that we can make in business is to reinvent the wheel, rather than pulling from our experiences. These experiences shape who we are, and what we can bring to the table. What we often fail to realize, is that experience creates experts, and we all have expertise in different areas. Your unique expertise becomes your differentiating factor and gives you a competitive advantage in the marketplace.

One of my best friends is an accountant. She has a unique skillset to break down figures and plan effectively. However, her passion is helping people. She gets a different level of joy from showing others that they're loved and getting them on the right track, almost like a life-coach. When she found purpose in her passion, it was difficult for her to focus on the therapeutic fluff that she assumed people needed from her. Until she realized that she could provide her mentees with a realistic audit of their lives and provide a calculated plan to turn certain things around. It was golden!

I had a similar experience. I love all aspects of business, but my background is corporate information technology and network marketing. I couldn't find a way to make the two relate when I began consulting. One aspect of my life focused on process automation and simplification, while the other was people driven. Sure, it makes sense now from a strategy and development standpoint, but it was difficult finding the correlation from the beginning.

I encourage you to take a step back and think about your area of expertise. How can your learnings and experiences give you a competitive advantage in your field? How can your skills improve your passions? How can your experiences dictate your actions? Give it some thought, and allow the expert in you to create a lane for your business in which no one else can compete.

# Thoughts

_____

_____

_____

_____

_____

_____

_____

_____

_____

_____

_____

_____

_____

_____

_____

_____

_____

_____

_____

_____

# 7

# Own It

There are three main things that I learned in corporate America, and each can be individually summarized by the same two words: OWN IT. Let's be honest ladies, many of us have the talent and skillsets to make us successful, but sometimes lack the confidence to make others believe it.

I struggled with this throughout my corporate and entrepreneurial career. Here I was, a young professional in a male-dominated industry. I was likely the daintiest employee in our information technology department. I spent my days in stilettos and pencil skirts in a building filled with crisp white collars and loafers.

I didn't fit in, and I hated it. I felt that they wouldn't respect me for me, so I toned it down quite a bit.

Guess what happened...nothing. I was so uncomfortable trying to make everyone else comfortable around me that I didn't bring my whole self to work, and it made me miserable. I spent more time thinking about reactions than I did thinking about excelling and it made me stuck. Finally, I realized that the only way I'd be the best me was to be the best ME. I went back to being myself, and my personality flourished. I was more comfortable talking to others, which made networking simple. More importantly, my confidence was reflected in my work. I knew what I was capable of and I proved it daily. They could hate on my heels, but they could never deny my work.

Now all of this sounds good, but there were a few steps that I had to take to get my confidence where I needed to be. First, I had to **focus on my strengths**. In other words, I had to recognize the exact table at which I was seated and what I could bring to it. Personally, I was an extrovert in an organization filled with introverts. I liked to get out and network while everyone else preferred to sit in their boxes. This allowed me to build relationships with my business clients that were unmatched by anyone else in my department. Next, I realized that I was a problem solver, not necessarily a "doer." I knew how to get things done, and relied on the relationships that I built with allies in my group to help me complete work much faster than others. Lastly, my colorful personality helped me bring a creative angle to the table that most technologists didn't see regularly. It was my competitive advantage, and I owned it!

I encourage you to consider your strengths. Ask yourself the following questions:

- What do you bring to the table?
- How do you uniquely solve problems?
- What do you see that others can't?
- What's your differentiating factor?

Take the time to think about your responses. No matter the environment, the answers to those questions will usually provide your competitive advantage over others. It certainly helped me to excel; then I focused on my second confidence creator: **personal presence**.

At some point in my career, I did an icebreaker exercise at a training event. Each student was required to stand and introduce themselves, while everyone wrote down one adjective that described the person based on their introduction. At the end of the introduction, all the cards were collected and given to the individual to illustrate how you "show up" to strangers. Here I am, expecting to see "fierce" and "feisty," but instead I got "warm, friendly, and bubbly." I find it comical that my mind saw sharp and intense, while the world saw fashionable, yet approachable. I wanted them to stand at attention, while they all wanted to hug me!

Why do I share this with you? It's simple, your presence isn't just about what you think, but how you show up. Could it be that your lack of confidence stems from the disconnect between how you see yourself vs. how you show up? Don't get me wrong, you never want to focus on the opinions of others, but it's important to acknowledge them if you expect those opinions to support you, buy into you, or buy from you.

Here are a few tips that helped me:

- **Say your name** – studies show that a person's favorite word is their name and the more it's heard, the more one's esteem is boosted. If you have to give a presentation or close a deal, try including your name in your affirmations. It'll spike your confidence to help you feel your best, so you can do your best.

- **Strike a pose** – Vogue? No. But, position your body with language that says authority. You'll usually find me sitting in the same position at all board meetings because it's my power pose. Adjust your body in a way that gives you both comfort and clout. For me, its legs pulled to one side and crossed at the ankle (feminine, yet professional). Hips to the back of the chair for comfort, back slightly leaned forward for engagement, chin tilted upward, eyes slanted, and an arm leaning on something so that it can be placed gently below my chin when I'm not speaking. This pose means that I didn't come to play. What's your power pose?

- **Know your Big Joker** – Spade's is my favorite card game, and even the worst player knows that having the Big Joker guarantees you at least one book. It trumps every other card that can be played at any given time. It may take some practice to learn to use it effectively, but the rules don't change. What's your trump card? What move, what phrase, what skill, what theory guarantees you the win? Think about it and use it as needed.

Your competitive advantage and your presence in any area of business will always be key components of your brand. Remember that a successful brand is dependent upon consistency. Be sure to represent that brand well at all times.

Lastly, owning it means taking responsibility. As a woman in business, you must take responsibility for your words, your actions, and your decisions. Celebrate your victories and take responsibility for your losses. Remember, as a Ladypreneur® you win or learn, never lose. However, you can't learn from mistakes where you make excuses or blame others. When you fall short, examine what could have been done differently, regroup, strategize, and try again.

Now let's focus on Rule #7, Balance!

# Thoughts

Juanika Dildy

# 8

# **Beaming Balance**

adies, what's the worst feeling in the world outside of stress or heartbreak? Feeling overwhelmed! Many of us cope with this as a part
of our everyday lives. As women, we're pulled in so
many different directions. We're mothers, we're
businesswomen, we're wives, we're community leaders,
we're spiritual partners, we're servants, we're counselors,
we're mentors, etc. With each hat, or heel in our case,
comes an equally different set of responsibilities, and jug-
gling them all at once can be overwhelming. I don't
understand anyone that juggles for fun. To be successful,
you must carefully plan out the timing of what you'll

throw and what you'll catch. If that timing shifts at all, you'll likely get hit in the head.

So, what's the answer? What will keep you from feeling overwhelmed? Balance? No! If you've ever watched a balance beam, you must constantly add and remove until the beams are stable. What does this mean? There's never 100%. Trying to balance means you give a percentage of yourself to your spouse, a percentage of yourself to your kids, to your ministry, to your business, and you never show up as a whole person to anything. What you need to do is learn to manage your time.

Years ago, I watched a video on time management by Franklin Covey. The goal was to fit different-sized rocks into a jar. Each participant that attempted failed because he or she always started with the smaller rocks. Once the smaller rocks filled the space, there was no room left for the larger rocks. On the final trial, the participant filled the jar with the larger rocks first, and the smaller rocks were able to fall into the crevices.

What's my point? Balancing your life, or managing your time is all about identifying your large rocks and tackling those first. In other words, plan out what's most important and let the rest fall where it can. If something has to shift, you won't feel overwhelmed because you've already handled what's most important. What are your large rocks? What are your non-negotiables? Is it your spouse, your children, your deadlines? Identify those things that absolutely must get done and give them your priority. You'll notice a change in your productivity and the overwhelmed feeling will disappear.

# Thoughts

# 9

# Directly Ask, Directly Tell

Grab a pen and write this down, **language matters**. In the world of business, the ability to effectively communicate can make or break you. If you can't illustrate your intent through words, your business is doomed. Let's resolve this together.

Write this down, **she that asks questions wins**.

Have you ever felt like you were backed into a corner trying to explain yourself to someone that was questioning you? I've witnessed it regularly and experienced it often in my own business. I have a friend that started a hair care line, and although her products are amazing, you could visibly see her confidence dwindle when she was bombarded with questions. Why? Not because she didn't know the information or was a bad communicator. Something about being questioned makes one defensive and when defenses arise, so do emotions. There's little room for emotions of that sort in business, so it usually causes defeat.

I know what you're thinking. How do you recover when bombarded with questions? Switch to the offensive line. Say what now? Flip it on them and ask your questions. Here's the key phrase,

"Let me ask you this."

This phrase will always position you to answer a question with a question and take back control. For example, if my friend was at a trade show and found herself questioned by a curious consumer, she may be hit with questions like "are these all natural ingredients" or "were the products animal tested?" A simple flip of "well let me ask you this, what do you prefer" or "let me ask you this, have you seen the article on…" will help her regain control of the conversation and provide information as the expert, not as one that's interrogated.

Next, **being direct eliminates assumptions**.

One can never assume what you mean when you tell them directly. Women, in particular, tend to struggle with concern about the response they'll get. Let me be the first to encourage you not to care. People will make up whatever storyline they choose if you allow it. Remove the ambiguity, say what you mean and mean what you say.

If you want someone to purchase, say it. If you want someone to take action, say it. The most successful method for direct language is the simple phrase,

"If I, would you?"

When someone questions your hair care line, you could easily respond by saying, "let me ask you this. If I answer your questions on the ins and outs of the product, would you be willing to try it for 10 days, risk-free?" Here you're communicating that you're willing to co-operate, with the expectation of action from them. Here are a few to have in your back pocket:

"If I explained the details of the business, would you be in a position to get started?"

"If I work this deal out for you, would you be ready to take action?"

"If I provided samples that you love, would you return to purchase?"

Phrases like these will help you communicate what you're willing to do and what you expect in return. This will provide clarity in your language.

Lastly, **have a tagline to resolve conflict**.

Unfortunately, we as women are deemed emotional because we fail to communicate through conflict effectively. When we react or fail to react, we're labeled with emotion, and I hate it. Here's what I did to avoid that label at all cost. Create a tagline that dismisses you from conflict. In other words, don't back down, but know when to agree to disagree. I've seen friends say things like, "miss me with that." This means I don't accept your position. Even Beyoncé and Angela Rye have often used the phrase, "boy bye," meaning I'm dismissing your opinion. I, however, love to say "I appreciate your passion, but…" This usually throws people off and gives me control of the conversation because I've subliminally called them loud and wrong.

Practice makes perfect. It doesn't matter what you say, as long as it's done professionally and with confidence. Write out pre-canned responses for things you find yourself addressing often. Write them down on notecards and practice if you must. Always listen effectively, but know how you'll respond. Continue to work on your language until you're able to find what works for you.

# Thoughts

# 10

# Close Deals in Heels

You may not wear heels at all times; that's fine. However, it is completely unacceptable in business to ever stop closing. I like to call it the ABC's of business – Always Be Closing. You get the point. Where there's no closing, there's no transaction. Where there's no transaction, there's no money. Where there's no money, there's no business. So, do yourself a favor and close close close!

First things first, know that some people aren't able to decide on the spot. Therefore, the win is in the follow-up. Make sure that you're getting contact information from potential customers so that you can build trust over time. Remember this, **people must like you and trust you, then they'll do business with you**. Find a channel of communication that will allow you to stay connected with the person. It could be email, text notifications, web-push notifications, etc. I prefer a mobile app (*download the* **'ladypreneur'** *app today in your mobile app store for the best training, building, and interaction among women in business!*), because we live in a mobile world.

Next, recognize that people will have questions. I'd have a 3-5 question rule to evaluate someone's interest. If a person isn't satisfied after you've answered 3-5 questions, provide them with documentation to read on their own, and enter them into your communication funnel to build trust over time. This will position you as the expert after some time has passed, and the person will come back with the intent to spend.

Lastly, remember to keep your language intact. Communicate your expectations by using, "if I, would you?" These statements will express your professionalism and eliminate assumptions.

# Thoughts

_____

_____

_____

_____

_____

_____

_____

_____

_____

_____

_____

_____

_____

_____

_____

_____

_____

_____

_____

_____

_____

_____

# 11

# Rest, Don't Quit

---

N ow that we've covered the fundamentals as women in business, let's focus on the absolute non-negotiables. I'm going to be completely honest with you; business is hard. Life as an entrepreneur can be scary. Leadership is uncomfortable. It will drain you physically, emotionally, and financially. If you're not careful, this roller-coaster ride will wear you out. However, it's important to acknowledge the fact that you will get tired. You'll feel like giving up, you'll feel like throwing in the towel. But when you're tired; rest, don't quit.

I failed fast and frequently early in my career. I made mistakes on all ends. I said the wrong things, reacted the wrong way, forgot key components, made the wrong decisions and it hurt me. I lost a lot of time, energy, and money, but I never gave up. My direction may have shifted as I learned from those mistakes, but I kept running. Why? Because quitters can't win, and winners can't quit.

I did competitive cheerleading as a young girl, and my coaches always reminded me of the importance of staying in the game. Coach Floyd, in particular, would remind us up front that we were going to fall. It was inevitable that we'd hit the ground. Sometimes it would hurt, we may bleed, we may even break something, but it was our responsibility to get our butts back up until we stuck our moves. I'll never forget the stunt we called the *Grin and Bear It*. Why? Because it took everything we had as a squad to get into that formation. It required strength and flexibility that didn't come easily. We had to bend in ways that we didn't usually bend, and utilize muscles we didn't even realize were there. It took twists and turns to get us there, but we smiled through the pain, and when it finally stuck, the crowd would roar!

There are some things that you'll have to grin and bear to be successful. When people don't support you, grin and bear it. When you're up late at night and early in the morning, grin and bear it. When you're overwhelmed because you've lost control of your schedule, grin and bear it. When you lose money, grin and bear it. When people talk about you, grin and bear it. When you have to miss birthdays, parties, baseball games, and recitals, grin and bear it. This thing called business is going to hurt, grin and bear it anyway. You're going to get tired, but I encourage you, Ladypreneur®; rest, don't quit.

# Thoughts

# 12

# Pay It Forward

I recently went on my first missions trip to Nassau, Bahamas. Now don't get me wrong, I'd visited Nassau before, but I'd never experienced it like this. My pastor warned me that it would be a life-changing experience, but I had no idea that it would have such an impact on my business.

I realized the importance of giving back in general, but it's deeper as a business owner. You see, the economy there is separated by those that work in the tourist industry. Those that worked for the major hotels, activities, clothing lines, casinos, etc. were considered middle to upper class. However, those that lacked opportunity fell below the poverty line. Unfortunately, this was most of the island. It didn't take me long to realize that we, as business owners, create the channels of opportunity that can change economic conditions. We facilitate the transactions that control the currency, but this is only one of many resources.

I encourage you today to use all that your business has afforded you to reach down and help others. Use your time, your money, and your influence to work on behalf of those that can't spend, speak, or work for themselves. Start locally, and build your way international. Identify the needs in your local area and position yourself to meet what you can. The government will support your contribution and reward your sacrifice. An even greater reward is waiting from God, who also honors your sacrifice. Consider what it took for you to achieve success, and help someone else. You'll stimulate growth and energize the community.

# Thoughts

Juanika Dildy

Thank you for hanging out with me, Ladypreneur®.
We wish you much growth and success, let's build!

Download the Ladypreneur® App today
from your mobile app store!

Available in App and Google Play stores

# Ladypreneur® Code – The Blog Series

Visit the Ladypreneur® App where you'll find
excerpts from our blog series in Ladypreneur®
Magazine! Here, we share personal entrepreneurial
experiences to help shape the mindset and behavioral
patterns needed to succeed in business ownership.
Several exclusive features have been made available
for Ladypreneur® Code – Rules of Engagement
for Women in Business.

# Who Told You You Were Naked?

N ow that I have your attention...HELLO LADIES! I want to personally welcome you to TheLadypreneur.com. This space was created specifically for the ultimate female entrepreneur. As we go throughout our journeys in our separate industries, we all have one thing in common...we're women on a mission!

Whatever that mission may be, it's important that we have a community that we can connect and share, learn and grow, laugh and even cry. Relationships are the currency of the kingdom, and if we're going to reach our God-given potential, it's important that we have a safe space to hold and be held accountable.

In my journey, I've seen many women with goals and dreams on the road to their destiny, and then it happens. The road that was once straight and narrow becomes rigid and curvy. The blue skies that originally created a zest and a zeal for our purpose quickly becomes dark and gloomy. Life hits us, and for whatever reason, it's hard to stand and run again.

I'm reminded of a familiar passage in Genesis (chapter 3). We all know the story...don't eat the fruit, they ate it anyway knowing HE would find out, they're ashamed so they cover themselves and hide, and HE comes looking. Now what happens next is what I wanted to share with all of you as we embark upon this journey together:

[9] God called to the Man: "Where are you?"

[10] He said, "I heard you in the garden and I was afraid because I was naked. And I hid."

[11] God said, "Who told you you were naked? Did you eat from that tree I told you not to eat from?"

Whether we realize it or not, the same mindset often plagues us thousands of years later. We fail so we hide, we get discouraged so we hide, our hearts are broken so we hide, we get rejected so we hide, things don't go as planned so we hide, we lose our balance so we hide. Often times a storm can feel like defeat, and defeat can leave us exposed...but, WHO TOLD YOU YOU WERE NAKED?

The same all-knowing God that created Adam & Eve was well aware of their shortcomings, but still asked the million-dollar question. Why? Because he didn't see them any differently than he did at the time of creation. So, I pose the same question to you, because it certainly applies. If God pre-planned for your storm, don't talk yourself out of your journey when the rain starts. Don't call yourself NAKED (i.e. defeated, a failure, discouraged, or fearful). It's time for us to rise up and take the world by storm.

I believe in you, and I encourage you to search your hearts today. Whatever vision that you were given to create in the world of entrepreneurship, decide that you're going to see it to the end. We're in this fight together, and I want to ensure that our heads are clear when we step in the ring!

You, sis, are not naked! You're beautiful, smart, creative, and a tad bit sassy. God loves it and so do I. Let's take this economy by storm and create a better environment for our future. I'm strapped up and ready to roll, are you ready for the ride?

# *Thoughts*

# Is Patience a Virtue in Business?

"Don't pray for patience!" I can recall every wise and experienced woman in my life telling me that at some point. The idea was that if you prayed for patience, you'd have to learn to cope with delay, which meant that you were inviting the waiting game into your life voluntarily.

I was no fool, and no one likes to wait, so I did as I was told. But, that didn't stop me from waiting on things throughout my life. You may or may not know my story, but I'm certainly not an overnight success. In fact, it took years as an entrepreneur for me to get into the flow of increase. Seven years, to be exact, before I reached a place of comfort. I was determined to work while I waited, so over the course of time, I tried/failed, tried/failed, and tried/failed some more.

I'm curious to know how many entrepreneurs, businesswomen, corporate professionals, ministers, or whatever would've turned around had it taken them seven years to see the fruit of their labor? It reminds me of the bamboo tree. We all know that bamboo is used in some of the sturdiest creations, but it takes forever for it to grow. A bamboo plant must be watered and nurtured for ~5 years before it begins to sprout. But, when the sprout happens, it only takes weeks for it to grow into a completely mature tree.

It's a cute story, but how many of you would actually nurture something that you can't see for five straight years? Imagine the frustration from wasted resources feeding and watering the dirt that is supposed to be your harvest. The truth is that this applies in many of our business lives today. Not only do most businesses fail their people within the first 3 to 5 years, but people fail their businesses within the first 3 to 5 years because they want fast fruit!

Here's what we overlook when we're focused on the sprouting process; THE ROOT. While we're crying over the leaf that we can't see, there are massive roots growing underneath the surface laying the foundation to sustain the amount of weight that it will eventually need to support. Truth be told, I wouldn't have been able to handle the levels of success in year one or year two. Why? I had not grown the capacity to be well planted through the storms that often accompany business. In other words, my roots weren't deep enough.

I didn't ask for it, but I learned the value of patience in business! Patience equals discipline, and discipline leads to sound decisions. Sound decisions will make or break your business. I'm certainly not risk adverse, but the ability to discern the difference between what looks good to you and what is actually good for both you and your business will completely change the game!

To make a long story short, WAIT! Don't forfeit your destiny by retreating too soon or by rushed, hasty decisions. Take the time to water your bamboo tree. You'll look up sooner than you think and you'll have the foundation to build a business that has the capacity to outlast your competition, because you're rooted in greatness!

***Psalm 27:14***

# Thoughts

# Be Misunderstood, It's Your Brand!

"Why are you starting a business," they said. "You're wasting your 'prime' years," they said. "You went to college," they said. "What about your master's degree," they said. "You're a corporate professional," they said. If your story is anything like mine, you've heard "them" say a lot about your decision to become an entrepreneur.

Let's be very clear here, there is a distinct difference between lacking clarity, and being misunderstood. Both deal with perception, which in many cases is reality. But, you can only control one, so that's where your focus should be!

I spent waaaayyyy too much time questioning the uniqueness of me simply because those closest to me didn't get it. I couldn't understand why. These were the people that knew me best, how could they not be on the same page? Why would they not support me? Why would those that should be my biggest cheerleaders try to discourage me? The questions sound rhetorical, but trust me, I wanted answers. It didn't take long for me to realize that people can only understand from THEIR LEVEL of perception. In other words, no matter what they see, some people will never be able to handle the reality of you! The best part is that it's ok. The ones that can are waiting for your uniqueness to emerge!

Don't try to fit a mold that others may create for you. You had a purpose long before they had an opinion. If God needed them on board to accelerate and promote you, they would have your revelation, but they don't! You've been given unique experiences to mold and shape your thoughts, ideas, and faith into the platform that will give you success. If you're in ministry, minister in your own lane, fearlessly. If you're an entrepreneur, run with your ideas like you'd run for your life (because you are)! If you're in fashion or beauty, beat that face/rip that runway/slay girl slay, like it's no one's business!

God gave you the gift. I happen to be the businesswoman that loves a high heel and a red lip, but can work a deal at the table, move an audience without touching them, and bring a fresh anointing to the boardroom without blinking. Why? Because that's the lamp-stand that God gave me to let my light shine! That's my brand, and it was birthed from my unique experiences!

Your job is to find your lane, be clear about your message, and be okay with being misunderstood. As long as you're true to who you are, success will find you!

\*\*Jeremiah 29:11\*\*

# Thoughts

_____

_____

_____

_____

_____

_____

_____

_____

_____

_____

_____

_____

_____

_____

_____

_____

_____

_____

_____

_____

_____

_____

# By All Means, Win!

"**Y**ou kinda look like Allyson Felix," the cashier shared as I approached the register. Flattered, I smiled and said thank you. Although I don't see the resemblance, an Olympic gold medalist has to have killer abs so I assume that's what she saw in me! Only in my dreams...

Either way, I was immediately reminded of the scene that's been replaying on every media outlet for the past 24 hours. Felix, on the verge of breaking the ultimate record for a female track runner, suddenly had it all snatched from her milliseconds from the finish line. At first glance, I was disappointed. This must be against the rules; clearly this other girl cheated; she was obviously desperate; etc. But at the end of the day, she took home the gold! If any rules were actually broken, Allyson would probably be smiling right now.

Two key terms should be noted here, STRATEGY and HUNGER. How many of us have the strategy to outwit our most fierce competitors? Many of us compete with businesses with higher clientele, maturer portfolios, and more brand recognition on a daily basis. Does that mean you rollover and let them win? Absolutely not! It's time for you to dig deep and win by any means necessary!

Allyson likely wanted the gold with everything in her, but what set her apart from her competitor was hunger. Allyson could probably see it, but Shaunae Miller could obviously taste it. Contrary to popular belief, skill never beats desire. So I must ask, how bad do you want success? Are you comfortable running with winners, or do you want it bad enough to take the gold?

The bible promises that we're:

The head and not the tail, above and not beneath, the lender and not the borrower - Deuteronomy 28:13

It's time for us all to take our dive! It's time we give it all we've got. Study your craft enough to challenge rules that most don't even know exist. Create your own lane and finish first. It's your season, it's your time...shine ladypreneur, shine!

# Thoughts

# The Power of Woman

cried like a baby. Because I'm a woman? Partially...but mainly because I'd just spent two hours in awe watching a film on three young African American women in a small city, only 25 miles from my hometown, that defied the odds against them and made astronomical advances for the great US of A. My tears were filled with pride as I watched these 'hidden figures' that looked like me, spoke like me, were feisty like me, and refused to take no for an answer, just like me.

Then today happened. I felt that same pride as I watched millions of women flood the streets in cities across the country taking a stand for their beliefs and making their voices heard. #Nastygirl, #Womensmarch, and #Marchforwomen posts consumed my feeds. I watched all colors and all ages unite with one voice, marching to the beat of one drum, and it hit me. Like a ton of bricks in that moment, I realized the power of woman.

WOMAN was what God created when nothing else was suitable for what he made in his image. WOMAN was what God intended to give birth and pro-create. WOMAN was what God created as a natural nurturer. WOMAN was created in his timing and with a purpose.

So ladies, it's time we take our place as the matriarchs of the marketplace. It's time we give birth to the seeds of ideas, dreams, and visions that he placed in our wombs. We're women of passion and purpose, and history can't be made without HERstory!

Moses wouldn't have a story without the woman that thought to spare his life. Samuel wouldn't have been the prophet that God trusted without the faith of the woman that fought through barrenness to finally give birth to him. An entire culture would've been wiped out without the courage of a woman that was loved by a Persian king.

In case you missed my point, we're here for a reason and the marketplace will never thrive without us. So go ahead and write that book, make that product, sing that song, give that presentation, live those dreams. Nothing can be birthed without your womb. It's our responsibility to pro-create. So let's pro-create change in our communities. Let's pro-create stability in our economies. Let's pro-create ministry in our markets and faith in our fields.

If it's to be, it's up to SHE. So get out there and give it all you've got!

# Thoughts

_____

_____

_____

_____

_____

_____

_____

_____

_____

_____

_____

_____

_____

_____

_____

_____

_____

_____

_____

# Experience A 2017, Like You've Never Seen

**H**appy New Year Ladypreneurs®! For some of us 2016 brought bountiful blessings and for others of us, 2016 came with a sucker-punch or two. Either way, if you're reading this, you're still here and it's not, so guess who won? You did!

Although I love the saying, "New Year/New Me" that takes the average person 1.5 months to forget, as if he or she had completely transformed from 11:59pm to 12:00am, that's not why I'm here. I've spent time reflecting on my year, as do many of us, and I'm inspired!

I compare my 2016 to that of my favorite Olympic track and field runner, Allyson Felix. This is a young lady who many of us witnessed her defeat, disappointment, tests and victories publicly! Not only did she exhibit her faith and wisdom during her trials, but in the end, she rocked her gold medals with pride! That type of excellence doesn't happen by chance. So, if Allyson and I could help you experience a 2017 like you've never seen, this is the advice we'd give:

**ON YOUR MARK:** Ladies, no one will ever win a race they don't show up to. Now is the time to map out exactly where you'll show up and stand out this year. It's time to write out your goals and make sure they have dates. A goal without a date is just a wish; now envision it!

My personal favorite method is through a vision board. Get yourself a poster-board, magazine cutouts, tape/glue, and go to work! Only you and God know exactly what you want out of this year and years to come, so write that vision and make it plain (Habakkuk 2:2)! Once you've finished, keep it in plain sight so that no one can deter or distract you from the goals you've set. Next up...

**GET READY:** Preparation is key! I've never seen a gold medalist that hasn't trained, nor will I ever see a consistently successful person that fails to prepare. Robert H. Schuller put it best by saying, "spectacular achievement is always preceded by unspectacular preparation." It may hurt, but you have to work those muscles so that they're ready for the big dance. No matter your course, read those books, study that craft, proof that presentation, perfect that product, or practice that pitch. Whatever you do, prepare!

**GET SET:** Now that you know where you're going and you've prepared for the journey, focus! The enemy of your life is so afraid of you actually making it to your destination and it's your job to beat him! Turn off the TV. Tell your friends you can't hang out tonight. Avoid the urge to scroll, tweet, post, or snap and sign off! 97% of the population fails to reach their dreams because of distractions. Put on your blinders and jump over to the 3%. Trust me, it's worth it!

**GO:** Take action! Don't be the person that's always getting ready to get ready. Don't think, do. Now is not the time to doubt or question yourself. God can't drive a parked car, so get in gear and get moving.

You have 365 days ahead to make 2017 a year like you've never seen. Everything you need is already inside of you. Don't waste it. You've got what it takes. You're a winner, a champion, and you will be successful if you move forward. You, my dear ladypreneur®, can do all things through Christ who gives you strength. Now get on your mark, get ready, get set, and GO!

# Thoughts

Juanika Dildy

Download the Ladypreneur® App today
from your mobile app store!

Available in App and Google Play stores